CU01433416

# Dear Diary

# PALMETTO
**P U B L I S H I N G**
Charleston, SC
www.PalmettoPublishing.com

Copyright © 2024 by Gabrielle Wilson

All rights reserved
No portion of this book may be reproduced, stored in a retrieval system, or transmitted in any form by any means–electronic, mechanical, photocopy, recording, or other–except for brief quotations in printed reviews, without prior permission of the author.

Paperback ISBN: 979-8-8229-4466-4
eBook ISBN: 979-8-8229-4467-1

# Dear Diary

GABRIELLE WILSON

# Contents

*Dear Diary,*

27 times around the sun and 2,700 lessons learned in love. I've experienced different types of love and crossed them off my list waiting to get what I deserve. Waiting hopelessly, turning a blind eye to the heartbreak to come after every failure. As I grew older, I grew in wisdom, I grew closer to God, but I'm still growing in patience. Because every time I fall for somebody, my hopes rise high like a thermometer in the mouth of a child with a fever. They get high and hot. OH MY GOODNESS! Could it finally be happening? But when my hopes are at their peak, I realized that some part of me needed to be healed and the temperature starts to decrease at the same time that the fire between me and whoever begins to dwindle. Sometimes I have no idea what went wrong and it leaves me permeated with questions. Through my healing process, I just have to accept that God called it off for reasons only He can see. Not because I did something to turn the person off. Not because I'm not good enough. Not because there was someone else. Not because I was no longer beautiful. Simply because it was not meant to be. Love and all its categories are so complex. I love my sisters like we each took a piece of each other's hearts in the place of our own. I love my friends like happiness loves a smile. I love my mom the way the moon loves the ocean, all the waves crashing and the tsunamis forming, and the hidden depths that it will never know. I love my daughter an unimaginable amount that sometimes it feels like there is nothing there at all because I am consumed by it. I want to love somebody the way that the rain loves the earth and the morning loves the dew. But more importantly, I want someone to love me the way that I seek and deserve.

# Dumb Jocks

*Dear Chase,*

Flowers have no choice but to be beautiful.
It has been written all through time.
And just as flowers blossom then die, you were once mine.
The last cool breeze before summer caresses you, kissing your skin goodbye.
Dancing in your hair carrying your aroma to the sky.
The breeze is no longer there at night to sing you a lullaby.
Only the stars to watch the regret fall from my eyes.

# Vulnerable

I hate that I am always thinking about you because it just makes me wonder if you're thinking about me.
And there is nothing scarier than the feeling of uncertainty.
Nothing is scarier than letting my heart take the lead when my head only gets in the game when this love game got me beat.
We both have a past so we know what to do in order to make this thing last.
I know exactly what I want but I get messages from my past that shout "don't move too fast".
Every second with you matches the rhythm of my heart
so I had to play it cool in order to give you a head start.
I fall hard and quick so I would've left you behind if it wasn't for the lessons I've learned that linger in my mind.
I used to play hard to get.
I made sure men knew I had options.
I tried to make you jealous like you weren't my number one option.
But why would I ever want to make you have to second guess?
Why would I ever want to play like you weren't the one making my heart beat out of my chest.
I'm all about you and I hope you're confident in that.
For you I'll wear my heart on my sleeve and the truth on my back.
And this is not Scooby Doo so please don't make me solve a mystery.
I'm not one to play games.
I'm not like that girl Daphnee.

*Dear Justin,*

The last time that I talked to you, it was hot outside.
Now the air is brisk and quiet.
My heart is beating slowly because it's affected by this cold and I feel
like I have no control over my soul.
When the sun was high and beating down on my skin, it left a golden
hue as pure as the love that I had for you.
In the summer heat, my skin is so moist and supple just the way it feels
when our godly parts come together.
The way my lipgloss melts reminds me of the juices running down my
fingers from a popsicle on a hot sunny day.
But I'm a woman now.
I know how to make my body sway along with the heat rays.
The way the heat radiated from the black pavement and mixed with the
heat radiating from within me because of the liquor made me feel like I
was dancing with the devil.
But in an innocent way.
Summer nights came and I could see all the stars and I imagined being
one.
I could whisper down to earth my words of wisdom and I'd burn bright
red like saffron.
Ready to bow down.
But just for you.

# Letter To My Ex,

I wish I would've taken you more seriously.
But then again, I wouldn't have gone through all the things that made
me me.
But then again, all of it hurt.
But then again, if we would've stuck it out, it still might have hurt but
at least I would have something to show for it. Sometimes there is so
much weight on my head too heavy that an Escalade couldn't chauffeur
it.
Like, what if I would have done this instead of that?
Or what if I would've curved Caleb instead of never calling Tai back.
Because what if freshman year I wasn't having the time of my life feel-
ing free of my momma's chains.
Taking full advantage of the better half of having beauty and brains.
Or so-called better half. Because if I was using my brains as much as I
was using my beauty, I wouldn't still be reminiscing thinking of what
could be.
And maybe you would've never heard my name in the football locker
room.
And maybe you would've gotten all my attention instead of me giving
some of it to Trey.
It's hard for me to say that I regret anything.
Still, I just can't help but wonder, if I had a second chance would you
even still see me the same way?

# Miss Me

Miss me like I'm the only girl that hits your line.
Miss me like I really ride for you so I sat and did some time.
Miss me like we in college and you in your dorm but I went back to mine.
Miss me like six miss nine.

# Dear John

# Every Boy I've Ever Loved,

I have fallen too deep and you watched me.
When you left I was down on my knees.
When you left I was down on my knees, looking up to sky child please.
I'm drowning in you. How could you leave?

You take over my thoughts and how I breathe.
I wear all your words on a sleeve.
My mind is always gone. I need relief.
But the thought of life without you hurts to receive.

I have fallen too deep and you watched me.
You made a fool out of me and you're laughing.
I'm the girl of your dreams. How could this happen?
This is a silent war. What am I lacking?

You take over my thoughts and how I breathe.
I'm so ashamed of myself. I've been so weak.
Some clarity is all that I need.
One more time you get to break me and I 'm free.

## Dear Caleb,

Before I closed my eyes at night, I talked to God about you.
Always thankful for all the things that you say and that you do.
Understanding who you were and how to handle all your pain.
I wish I knew to walk away before you took away my name.
Before you took away my sanity and labeled me insane.
Had me wishing that your momma never wrapped your heart in chains.
She must've been a broken woman because she broke you.
And now you can't man up and do the things a man should do.
Understand that I was down.
You must have never had a clue just what love felt like because I gave my all to you.
You took your anger out of context and you let the coward show.
And the crazy thing is that I couldn't let you go.
You broke my heart and I let you.
I didn't learn anything. I wish I never met you.
You'll never find anyone like me
But I'll find a man better than you.

*Dear Caleb,*

I took a breath without you and it threw me for a loop.
Because it all rushed in so quickly, I had to take a minute to recoup.
All the life that I was missing,
I had forgotten how to breathe.
I hadn't realized that loving you took my breath and brought me to my knees.
My chest was weighed down by painful interactions that still bring sweet memories.
I was blinded by your love but we still embraced each other so confidently.
With all the effort I could muster, I loved you still.
Even when it felt like every dance was meant to kill.
You were mine until you werent.
I was always yours.
I was stranded on an island and you were nowhere to be found
so I swam across an ocean and it caused my heart to spin around.
I miss the nights when we were together floating in the stars but I had to let go of you.
You created too many scars.

# In My Feelings

# Save Me From Myself

Save me from myself again and the dreams I have that lead me to sin and the nightmares that make me question all that I have within. And even though it's a scary dark path, I take it again and again. As long as it puts a smile on my face in the end. So save me from myself. From the enemies that became my friends. From the evil smirk that has no end. Light was once my lover. She caressed me with a warmth that left me smiling in my sleep and when the sun came up, I was lost in my daydreams still counting sheep. As the clouds rolled by and carried my tears and the sunset took me back to a time when I had no fears. But in the dark, dreams turn into nightmares where I look in a shattered mirror and try to save me from myself again. There's so many stars that flutter in space at night so I'm mesmerized by their soft light. And like a wish, my sins float up to the black sky and you can see their beauty reflecting in my eyes. So when God spins the earth, I feel the heat of the sun and I look up to find shapes in the clouds and something deep inside me becomes aroused. So save me from myself. From the voices in my head and the evil laugh that mocks me when I go to bed. All the beauty in the world laughs at the things that are dead.

# Nightmares

I trusted you with my nightmares.
Curled up on your chest like a toddler waiting for you to check for monsters.
Then I gave you my dreams and under the night sky we'd sing.
I was hopeful for all the things our melody would bring.
I was submerged in the ocean deep hiding from the hurricane on its way to our seas.
But lightning struck leaving a familiar mark.
I just hope to remember the feeling I felt.

# I'll Be Right Back

If I'm being honest my patience is wearing thin.
And it's hard because I know that you're being the best man that you can.
Right now I'm being tested.
But I know more than I ever did so this could be forever.
Longer than the loves that never lasted.
I'm just trying to trust that what we have is sent from above.
Trying to find peace in every struggle before I take off the gloves.
Love is a choice and I need to start choosing me that way i'm not crying into my diary.
So I'll be right back where you need me.
Right back to when our words were pretty.
Right back to when we were both sturdy.
But I'm gone. I'm going home back into my fathers arms because I took my focus off of Him and that only ever causes harm.

# Growing and Glowing

Then I decided to go through life blind. The ocean and the sky are in love with each other and kiss at the end of each day. I want my life to be surrounded by love and for love to flow through me. So I lay on the water and all of me drifted together and apart. The water splashes over my eyes. Then I decided to go through life silently. I listened for the sounds of my breath and discovered beneath the surface, my thoughts are free. I threw my head back and let the water carry it. Then I decided to go through life with love. So I looked up at the sky and floated to cloud 9. That's where I found a piece of me. I allowed myself to think more creatively and now I have no enemies. I looked back into the water and saw myself. Then I looked at my watch and it was 3am.

# Surrender

Letting go of you hurts more than being let go of.
It's the pain ice brings when you're fully submerged.
And I wasn't ready to be in a room full of people and still feel alone
faced with the hardest part of life cause I'm young but I'm grown.
My mind is always crowded, my vision always blurred.
Who knew the fog could get this dense.

# Ballerina

Lately, she's been dancing with the devil.
She's never felt anything that was heavier.
But she carries the weight the way a ballerina rises to her tippy toes and dances around like a feather.
Or the way your body moves freely underwater.
The whole time, her lungs are being crushed by the pressure.
She lights up the room the way the sun peeks through your blinds in the morning and opens your eyes.
And when she parted her lips to giggle, you were in for a sweet surprise because her smile was just as beautiful as the sun's early dawn rise.
As calm as the sea with a force so powerful it'll leave you gasping for air.

# 3am

From out of the earth comes a woman.
Pain was something she knew too well as if it was preached to her every
day like a sermon.
Knocked down by the winds of uncertainty and planted like a seed.
She was dancing in the fire. A sinner's creed.
From out of the water comes a soul.
Dripping off her body were the things that made her whole.
She liked the way the earth felt on the bottom of her feet.
So when she dreamt at night, she waited for a place where her and God
could meet.
From out of the flower comes the divine,
Looking up in the clouds for a sign.
Every morning, she woke up with the sun.
The dirt that burdened her was all done.
From out of the sun comes the light.
Its energy was so strong that the soul was lifted and took flight.
By the time I was standing on my own two feet,
Heaven met me and I was complete.

# New Balance

Your touch feels like summer.
Clear my mind but leave some room for wonder.
I was lost
But in this ocean, keep me anchored through the days.
Flow through me just like the waves.
This new beginning , like the sunrise each day, has my heart pumping
blood in a new way.
Don't forget about life.
Don't forget about sleepless nights sometimes walking through the
storm without even putting up a fight.
But this new melody is dancing around me like a summer breeze.
You give me a feeling like I'm thinking of all the birds and all the bees.
While keeping control of my soul, fill me with warmth and never let
go.

# YAHWEH,

You make me appreciate the sunsets more and the way they make me feel.
I want to dive deep into the flower beds and feel your rivers flow.
My entire being absorbs every part of you just like the way the sun kisses me and leaves that golden dew.
I dream about you.
And when I open my eyes your light shows me a path that allows me to surrender all my might.
Without you, I wouldn't know what to do.
Your light surrounds me.

# Complicated Situations

# Leverage

Let's just be nothing. I heard that nothing lasts forever.
Going in circles I should've left when I knew better.
I'm not your everything but I still fold under pressure.
You take all that I am and you morph it whenever.

All that I am and all the love that I give.
I'm not as strong as I can be because I think your attention is a privilege.
I trifle with the specks of happiness you give and use it as leverage.
For the next girl, I hope you take away from this. I'm learning lessons.

Pretty please.

# Back and Forth

Her: I really wish you'd stop lying to yourself.
Him: I know it breaks your heart. I'm lying to the both of us and I blame myself for the vulnerability that I withheld.
Her: In the past, I've seen too much to stay now. I have to put me first now. I have to throw in the towel.
Him: But I don't feel like I'm winning-
Her: And I don't feel like I have much to show for all the feelings we let grow.
Him: Now I'm feeling all the emotions that you let go of.
Her: Does it hurt? I hope it hurts. So you come running back. Baby I'll take you back.
Him: Then maybe I should stay away because I don't want to break your heart. I'm not the man you need and it makes me feel weak.
Her: I hate it when you talk like that. I fell for who you are and not who you could be.
Him: Baby I'm just not ready.
Her: You can't even tell me why I hate that you're so blind. I'd wish you'd just open your eyes. You know I'll always love you. But I can't say that I'll always want you. I wish that I could make you see. I wish that I could make us be. But I have to move on...
Him: Wait...

*Dear Barry,*

Two months ago we were sitting at the bar and I was eating off your plate while laughing in each other's face. Reminiscing about our first date.

Two months ago I was confident that I was done having to wait. Done learning lessons and sleeping next to mistakes.
With you, everything just fell into place.
I could look into your eyes and see that God was working on a masterpiece.

One month ago, I got over you and healed all my scars.
How we ended makes me realize you never even cared about me at all.
You're not welcome back into my life.
But you calling me now makes me hope just a little that we were just meant to do this twice.

So I just don't understand when the switch up occurred .
And I don't think you realized how confusing it was when suddenly the idea of wanting us to last forever sounded absurd.

# Wasting Time

Did I fall so hard again that I forgot to check the clock?
Spending all this time just to end up blocked and spending all my
emotions just to end up clocked.
At the end of it all a judge couldn't even place the blame.
Nowhere to hide from all of the shame.
Kept holding on ignoring this silly game.
You don't know what you want so you say anything that gives you con-
trol over my name.
Not letting go even after realizing the love won't remain.
And I hold on  maybe because I'm scared of the pain.

*Dear Jonah,*

When you talk to me like that I just hope that you mean it.
My love is innocent so when you look into my eyes I just hope you see it.
I know what type of man I want. I just hope that you can be it.
You just know what sounds nice. I just hope I can see it.

The chemistry was beautiful. I just hope that we can keep it.
This could be something real. I just hope that we achieve it.
You say that you can give me everything I dream of so I just hope that you can prove it.
You've never proved it in the past. I just hope I can see it.

*Dear Barry,*

Even after all that, I really did miss you.
Besides, every relationship has to overcome different issues.
And I realize now that I was in a rush.
I just need to take some time to focus on myself but still linger in your touch.
You're still becoming the man you want to be.
And I don't want to get in the way of that because your growth will also benefit me.
I know that sounds selfish but I'm a woman and I have needs.
I just hope you know that I'm willing to play my part and give you a different type of peace.
The unspoken expression that we use to give love is strongest when I'm with you.
You helped me to realize that in the past I was misused.
But your language is touch just as much as mine is.
The only distinction is that I like to give and you like to receive.
That's the type of balance that I seek.
You're the man I pray about before I go to sleep.
Your entity is something that I need.

# Cast Away

The wind blows free just the way love escapes from my body.
Fighting it brings sorrow to my soul.
Freeing it tightens my chest and makes it hard to breathe.
Hurt shortly follows
because my love always finds gates it can't enter, hearts it can't reach,
souls that attract each other but then crumble at the peak.
I have loved in every life.
Cast it out like a bottle in the ocean only for it to find its way back to
me withstanding treacherous seas, witnessing beautiful sunrises and
then sunsets. Mending itself back together under God's eyes.
I have waited and I will wait
until my love has answered its fate.

Milton Keynes UK
Ingram Content Group UK Ltd.
UKHW030831260824
447446UK00002B/254

9 798822 944664